MW00389768

The
TWO-
MINUTE Drill
to PARENTING

MOLDING YOUR SON INTO A MAN

JOHN CROYLE

FOUNDER OF BIG OAK RANCH

LifeWay Press®
Nashville, Tennessee

The Two-Minute Drill to Parenting
Published by LifeWay Press®
© 2014 John Croyle

ISBN: 978-1-4158-7810-1
Item: 005558746

Dewey Decimal Classification Number: 649
Subject Heading: PARENTING \ SONS \ PARENT-CHILD RELATIONSHIP

Unless otherwise indicated, all Scripture quotations are taken from the Holman Christian Standard Bible®, copyright © 1999, 2000, 2001, 2002 by Holman Bible Publishers. Used by permission.

Scriptures marked NIV are taken from the Holy Bible, New International Version, copyright © 1973, 1978, 1984 by International Bible Society. Used by permission.

Scriptures marked MSG are from The Message, copyright © 1993, 1994, 1995, 1996, 2001, 2002 by Eugene Peterson. Published by NavPress. Used by permission.

To purchase additional copies of this resource:
ORDER ONLINE at www.lifeway.com;
WRITE LifeWay Small Groups; One LifeWay Plaza; Nashville, TN 37234-0152;
FAX order to 615.251.5933
or PHONE 800.458.2772

Printed in the United States of America

Adult Ministry Publishing
LifeWay Church Resources
One LifeWay Plaza
Nashville, Tennessee 37234-0152

CONTENTS

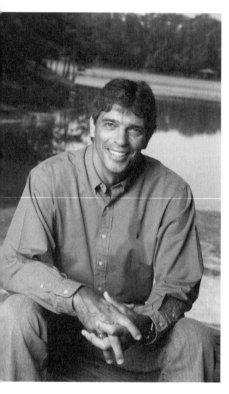

ABOUT THE AUTHOR

John Croyle, founder and executive director of Big Oak Ranch, was a defensive end for the University of Alabama's 1973 National Championship football team, playing for the legendary Coach Paul "Bear" Bryant. At age 19, John felt he had been given a gift to work with young people. His dream was to have the best children's home in America. On the advice of Coach Bryant, John declined opportunities to play professional football and instead chose to pursue his dream of helping children in need.

John established Big Oak Boys' Ranch in 1974. Today Big Oak Ranch, Inc. has grown to include Big Oak Girls' Ranch and Westbrook Christian School. John and his wife Tee have helped raise nearly 2,000 children through Big Oak Ranch as well as their biological son Brodie, a former NFL quarterback, and daughter Reagan, a former basketball player at the University of Alabama.

John's philosophy can be summed up in this statement: "A hundred years from now it will not matter what my bank account was, the sort of house I lived in, or the kind of car I drove ... but the world may be different because I was important in the life of a child" (Forest E. Witcraft).

The cornerstone and even the name of Big Oak Ranch is fundamentally rooted in Isaiah 61:3, "They will be called oaks of righteousness, a planting of the LORD for the display of his splendor" (NIV).

Today John, wife Tee, and children Brodie and Reagan, along with the Big Oak Ranch staff, continue to meet the needs of hundreds of children by giving them a solid Christian home and a chance to fulfill God's plan for their lives.

A MESSAGE FROM JOHN

Welcome to *The Two-Minute Drill to Parenting*! I know what it feels like to play under a good coach. He has a game plan, and he is focused. When he steps onto the field, he wants to lead his team to victory. It's that simple. Winning the game is reward enough for all the long hours of practice. The drills, the heat, the pace, the intensity—week after week, coaches lead their teams in practice until they are ready for game day, until they are ready to win.

As parents, we want our boys to grow up and be men, but we need to have a game plan as well. It won't happen by accident. We need to be focused and ready to lead and launch our sons into authentic manhood. If we can see the big picture, develop a strategy, count the cost, remain consistent, and live it out at home, our sons will be ready to step onto the field of manhood.

But it all starts with us.

In football, the two-minute drill prepares the team to be focused and ready for the final minutes. If executed correctly, it can make or break a team. As parents, we need to ask ourselves a very important question: *What strategies are we going to develop and execute at home so that our boys can step into manhood and make it?* It's crucial that we answer this question to give our sons the best shot at succeeding as men.

In my time at Big Oak Ranch, I've watched boys turn into men right before my eyes. Big Oak Ranch is a living testimony of God's goodness and faithfulness. It represents nearly 40 years of experience raising abused and neglected boys. I've seen first-hand the positive effects of having a path to manhood and leading boys to embrace it. I know the importance of keeping your eye on the clock because time is ticking.

I want to thank you for allowing me to share my experience with you. Consider this resource your coaching guide—from one coach to another. I hope it helps you keep your eye on the clock, too, as you lead your son down his path to manhood.

John Croyle
Founder of Big Oak Ranch

HOW TO USE THIS STUDY

We're glad you have chosen to study *The Two-Minute Drill to Parenting*! As this study guides you through a game plan to help ensure your son is ready for authentic manhood, it is our prayer that you will not only feel empowered to become a more godly influence in the life of your son but you will also experience a closer relationship with him as you share this journey together. Before you get started, here is some helpful information about the different elements you'll encounter within the study.

Week Introduction

Each session begins with an overview of the week's topic. This material is designed to introduce you to the content you will study that week. Reading the introduction before your group meets will help you better understand the topic and the context for your time together.

Huddle Up: Review

This time is designed to provide you with an opportunity to talk about what God has been revealing to you or what insights have resulted from your personal time during the week.

Huddle Up: Preview

This section provides questions or discussion starters designed to help you get familiar with the specific theme of the session and become more comfortable with discussion.

Video Discussion

This section provides an overview of what you will experience through the video message as well as discussion questions related to its content. This is an opportunity for the group to discuss specific aspects of the message, what you heard, and how you were affected.

Small-Group Discussion

This portion of your weekly group meeting will not only reinforce the video content but also take you deeper into the truth of the Scriptures. This segment of the study also gives you an opportunity to integrate these truths into your own parenting.

Highlights

This section serves as a conclusion to the group time and summarizes key points from your small-group meeting each week.

Execute the Play

At the end of each session you will find a suggested activity to complete during the week. This activity is an opportunity to take what you've learned during your small-group meeting and apply it. You may be asked to involve your son or to complete an activity in preparation for a future conversation with him. During your next group meeting you will have time to share some of what you've learned with your group.

Know that as we prepared this study we were praying for you. It is our hope that God will truly bless you on your journey to better prepare your son for the game of life.

THE GAME PLAN

WHAT COULD BE MORE REWARDING than knowing you have launched your children into the world prepared and ready? Just think about the personal satisfaction of leading them through the practice fields of adolescence and young adulthood before they venture off. Like a confident coach getting his team suited up for the big game, you will witness your boys preparing and suiting up for life.

As your boys grow into full adulthood, you will move more and more into a coaching role. But you need to see yourself as the coach who is preparing them for life even now. You have a God-given sphere of influence over your children. And since God trusts you with their lives, you need to know the steps, the drills, and the game plan. I know a lot about football, parenting, and boys! I know firsthand the kind of diligence necessary for preparing boys for manhood. I understand the sense of urgency you may be feeling—especially as you see your young boys grow up, hit puberty, start driving, start dating, ... Whoa, stop!

Actually, you can't stop, and that's the point. The clock is ticking and your boys need you more than ever. It is up to you. No one else knows your boys like you do. No one else has a sphere of influence over them like you do. From one parent to another, consider this series my personal invitation to you. And for this first session, let's talk about who you are and how you can fashion a game plan for the young men in your life.

The **Two-Minute Drill** to Parenting

HUDDLE UP

PREVIEW

■ *Use the following questions to kick off your small-group meeting. Start thinking now about what it means to have a game plan for your son as he begins to enter manhood.*

> "Practice does not make perfect.
> Only perfect practice makes perfect."
>
> VINCE LOMBARDI

What do you think Coach Lombardi meant by this statement?

What point do you think he was trying to make as it relates to preparation and winning?

Your home is the best practice field for your boys before you send them off to the big game of life. To what degree have you considered this truth? How intentional have you been in creating a "practice field" mentality at home for your son?

On a scale from 1 to 10, describe the *sense of urgency* you feel to do this parenting thing right.

1   5   10

Not at all   Very much so

VIDEO DISCUSSION

In this week's video you will get a glimpse into what having a game plan for taking your son from boyhood to manhood looks like. I'll be talking a little about what a parent is and what a parent is not. But you'll also hear from Eathan and hear about his experience at the ranch. My wife, Tee, will address areas of discipline and how to parent every minute of every day. We want you to get a good idea of how to create an effective game plan before we move into the heart of our group experience.

■ **Play Video 1: The Game Plan (10:53)**

■ *If your group is large, break into smaller groups of three or four to discuss the next two questions. Encourage group members to write down their personal takeaways as others share insights, stories, struggles, or victories.*

Throughout the video, Tee talks about the necessary decision to parent every minute of every day, even though you may grow tired and weary. What are some of the consequences of not sticking to God's minute-to-minute game plan?

The statement was made in the video, "Parenting is not the same as being a friend." Why do you think Tee would feel compelled to make this statement?

■ *Bring everyone back together as a large group to continue your discussion.*

Think about my two-minute drill concept for parenting. You practice, practice, practice, so when it's game time everyone knows the plan by heart. What do you consider your biggest obstacle to preparing your boys with this kind of parenting approach?

You're going to see that this study has a very hands-on approach to preparing your son for manhood. My experience at Big Oak Ranch has taught me a lot about boys. But my experience with God through His Word has taught me a lot about life. It doesn't matter how many obstacles you think you have in your way, you can develop a plan that's right for your son. As we turn to God's Word, let's look at what it's going to take to prepare our boys for the real world.

SMALL-GROUP DISCUSSION

There is a stark contrast between what you want your children to experience and what you know your children will experience when they leave home. This presents you with an unmistakable fork in the road for your boys. They will need to know the clear-cut path toward true manhood while navigating through a godless culture. Think about the reality check your son is going to experience when he leaves home and enters the real world for the first time.

Read 2 Timothy 3:1-5. This passage comes from Paul as he writes to young Timothy one last time. There's a special kind of character needed when we live for God in a godless culture.

In your own words, describe the kind of culture about which Paul warned Timothy. What do you think is at the heart of Paul's warning to Timothy?

How has your family been confronted with this sort of influence from the world?

Why do you think Paul's warning might be uniquely important to a boy who will someday be a man?

Throughout his ministry, Paul exemplified a very unique life. He related to people in different ways for different reasons. At one time he saw himself as a loving, nursing mother (see Galatians 4:19), and at other times he felt like he was a spiritual father (see 1 Corinthians 4:14-17). His motto was, "I have become all things to all people, so that I may by every possible means save some. ... I do all this because of the gospel" (see 1 Corinthians 9:22-23). As a parent, you have the freedom to:

- Be yourself. Don't try to be someone else.
- Be who your son needs you to be. Don't give up as you swap hats and are stretched in every direction.
- Do whatever it takes to climb into your son's world. As your son changes, you change right along with him.

GOAL

If you read the Gospels from a harmony perspective, you can see a hands-on approach in Jesus' method of training His disciples. He would send His followers out two-by-two and let them learn from experience. Jesus made Himself available and used real life to teach His disciples. Your parenting approach should be the same. Become more aware of the opportunities that real life affords you. Be intentional with your boys. Give them a real relationship with you. Offer them a real experience so God can shape them, and you can send them out.

Now read 2 Timothy 3:10-17. Regardless of the culture, Paul seems to be somewhat optimistic that Timothy is equipped to live out his godly manhood with a good example.

Paul knows that Timothy has experienced something different. Based on 2 Timothy 3:10-17, what do you think has given Paul hope that Timothy would be able to live as a "man of God" in such a culture?

The operative pronoun in this passage is *my*. Paul says to Timothy, "You have followed my teaching, conduct, purpose, faith, patience, love, and endurance, along with the persecutions and sufferings" (v. 10-11). Paul had a game plan for discipling Timothy. What is your game plan for using your life experiences to disciple your son?

Paul very pointedly refers to the Scriptures in these verses. What can you do in the next six months of your son's life to make the Scriptures more a part of his story?

"As parents, we must know who we are, what we are, and why we're here. Those are three bedrocks of parenting. They are just like the three sides of a pyramid or three legs of a stool. If two sides are the same length and the third is different, we will always be out of balance."

THE TWO-MINUTE DRILL TO MANHOOD

Highlights

- Your son needs you parenting him "every minute of every day."
- You cannot forget your identity and ultimate purpose as a parent.
- Your son needs an intentional relationship that allows him to experience you.
- Remember, you are not his friend. You are his parent.

EXECUTE THE PLAY
PLAN A TRANSITION TRIP

When the whole M.A.N.H.O.O.D. concept was taking shape, I was planning a "transition trip" with my son Brodie. I wanted a special time where I could talk to him, one on one, about what it means to be a man. And God provided a way for us to go to Alaska on my shoestring budget. That was a great experience. Not just the destination itself, but the entire journey—how we got there and what we experienced together.

Parents, you need to start thinking about a transition trip of your own. Don't talk with your son yet. Instead, sit down on your own and start thinking about it. When the time comes for you to have a discussion with him, he will definitely have some ideas of his own. But if you do some homework first, you will be prepared and ready to have this conversation. You will already have some ideas and options and will be ready to steer the conversation with some wisdom and "directed discovery" already in play.

These two pages will guide you through the logistics. Fill in each area as best you can. Be ready to discuss and share with your group the next time you meet. Sharing ideas and listening to the wisdom of others will help you as well.

What is your objective for the trip?

What are some possible/potential destinations?

Local Options:

Intermediate Options (drivable distance—up to 500 miles):

Extensive Options (requiring air travel):

What is a realistic budget?

• **Travel**

Gas

Airfare

Hotel

Food

• Entertainment

Gear

Excursions

Reservations

Guides

Throughout the remainder of this study, fill in some key thoughts or ideas that you would like to communicate to your son on your transition trip.

• Master

• Ask and Listen

• Never Compromise

• Handle Your Business

• One Purpose

• One Body

• Don't Ever, Ever, Ever Give Up

M=
MASTER

If you liked to read when you were growing up, you probably had a favorite book series. There's one series I remember that actually let you "choose your own adventure." To a certain degree, you were given control over how the story unfolded.

But here's an interesting thought. You don't have control over the outcome or events of the book, just the choices that the main character will make. And even still, you're bound by the guidelines and limitations the author has set. This isn't a free for all. You still have boundaries.

When it comes to choosing the right master, our lives are a lot like these books. We have free will. We make choices every day, and those choices determine much of who we are. But we also have limitations. We aren't perfect. We can't control everything around us. We aren't writing our own script as we go. We have boundaries.

We make choices that will determine the course of our future. But those choices also reveal who is the real master of our lives. Parents, your boys are paying attention more than you think. Together, let's learn how to lead our sons to choose the right kind of Master for their lives. As the foundational step in developing M.A.N.H.O.O.D., it's crucial that they get this right from the very beginning.

HUDDLE UP

REVIEW

■ *Use the following questions to kick off your small-group meeting by reviewing the ideas group members came up with for a transition trip, as well as things the Lord has revealed to them over the past week about relating to their sons.*

What ideas did you come up with for your transition trip? Did you get stuck? Ask the group to help. Sharing ideas will help you develop your plan even more. Use the space below to take notes of ideas and wisdom shared by other group members that might be helpful to you as you continue to plan for your trip.

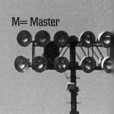

PREVIEW

■ *Use the next few minutes to answer the following questions as a small group. It will help you get the conversation going about what it means to have a Master.*

Which of the following would you desire to master the most? Choose from the list below or add your own.

The art of public speaking
Martial arts
Culinary arts
Gardening and horticulture
Outdoor adventure
Team sports
Writing and publishing
Other: _____

Most of these pursuits would be classified as "arts" because, even though they may not involve a literal canvas, mastering them paints a picture to those around you. If you were going to master something on a spiritual level, what would you want to pursue? Why?

LifeWay

Big Oak Ranch

KICKOFF

VIDEO DISCUSSION

In this video you're going to see the importance of your role as a parent in helping shape the choices your sons will make. I'll be talking about the three most important people you should love. You'll hear some of our houseparents talk about obedience to God and modeling Christ in front of your kids. My daughter, Reagan, discusses the impact my decisions had on her while growing up at Big Oak Ranch. My wife talks about the stresses and challenges of walking by faith—trying to follow God's call to run the ranch and how that faith-walk affected our kids growing up. All of this discussion, though, revolves around how we tried to apply and model the truths found in Matthew 6 and Romans 6. Both of these passages talk about choosing the right master for your life.

■ **Play Video 2: Master (11:09)**

■ *If your group is large, break into smaller groups of three or four to discuss the next two questions. Encourage group members to write down their personal takeaways as others share insights, stories, struggles, or victories.*

At the beginning of the video, Reagan talks about how obedience to the Master is what brings true spiritual contentment. Who modeled true contentment for you when you were growing up? Explain.

You also heard discussion of the false notion that being mastered by God is something negative when it's really not. In what ways do our culture, spiritual upbringing, or way of life at home play into this false notion?

■ *Bring everyone back together as a large group to continue your discussion.*

> **When Tee spoke about the challenges of walking by faith because of the nature of Big Oak Ranch ministry, I know she wasn't alone. You don't have to be involved in a faith ministry to struggle. What are some of the challenges you encounter when trying to walk by faith and follow God? (They could be personal, relational, vocational, etc.)**

If you haven't already noticed, you're going to see that preparing your son for M.A.N.H.O.O.D. rests more on you modeling it for him than you just teaching it to him. It's important that we pay attention to the details and consequences of our choices and actions. *Choosing* a master is a verb. It's not what we think about God, it's how we live our lives before God (and our sons). Our actions are tangible things that our boys see everyday. Your kids don't always know what you're thinking, but they can always see how you're acting. Let's partner together and encourage one another as parents. We can walk by faith, please God, and show our boys what it means to be mastered by God.

SMALL-GROUP DISCUSSION

Mastering something takes years of training and a heart of determination. There is a raw talent that is needed at first. But practicing day after day will develop that raw talent into a skill set that becomes second nature. What you have mastered will naturally become an extension of what you do and who you are. But what about *being* mastered by something or someone in the same way? Instead of raw talent, it takes a surrendered heart. Obeying day after day will develop that surrender into a skill set that will become an extension of what you do and who you are.

Read Matthew 6:24. When Jesus was talking about storing up treasure, kingdom life, and pursuing true happiness, He made a very definitive statement about the true nature of choosing a master. Even though Jesus specifically mentions money, the principle is the same, because money represents the pursuit of everything else.

Talk about the conflict you experience when you try to serve two masters. How have you experienced this tension in your life?

How does this tension spill over into your family relationships with your spouse or children?

Of all the things that can get in the way of God being our true Master, which one do you think your son picks up on most? (For example, is it how you spend your money, or where you spend the most time, or how you treat others?)

So many interests compete to be master of your life as a parent. How does Matthew 6:24 help you manage the kind of balance required to move your son along the path of manhood?

"We can't choose our child's master; our child has to choose. However, you can model the best choices for them, knowing that they will make some mistakes along the way. You won't win by judging, condemning, or blindly condoning their choices."

THE TWO-MINUTE DRILL TO MANHOOD

Read Romans 6:11-14. In this passage Paul is talking about how we have power over sin and that sin is no longer our master. But the choice is still ours to make, and it's a daily choice.

"Do not let sin reign in your mortal body, so that you obey its desires. And offer any parts of it to sin as weapons for unrighteousness. But as those who are alive from the dead, offer yourselves to God, and all the parts of yourselves to God as weapons for righteousness" (Romans 6:12-13). How can you best apply this principle to your role as parent to your son?

What do you think stands to be learned from your own efforts at making God your Master as it relates to you as a parent?

GOAL

Jesus obeyed His Father from the very beginning. As Jesus learned from His Father, He taught His disciples. Toward the end of His life, Jesus said, "I do not call you slaves anymore, because a slave doesn't know what his master is doing. I have called you friends, because I have made known to you everything I have heard from My Father" (John 15:15). As a parent, you submit to God's leadership and learn what it means to be mastered by God. As He teaches you to lead your family, you pass that along to your boys. And one day you can say, "I no longer just see you as my child, but as my friend, submitting to and learning from God together."

In the video, Reagan recounts the slogan I always used. "Let the Master of masters master that which is mastering you." It's just my way of pursuing what Paul is teaching here in Romans.

> **Inventory your life and your priority decisions. Acknowledge where those decisions are leading your family. Who's in charge of your life and what are you teaching your boys in the process?**

> **If your son chooses the same path, where will that path take him?**

The Scriptures are clear. In life you have two choices—either God will be your master or you will be your own master. One choice brings life, and the other choice brings death. Choosing God brings life and devotion. Choosing self brings death and destruction.

Highlights

- *Master* is the first step in developing manhood. When you get the Master part right, manhood will follow.
- Your attitude toward God speaks as loudly as your actions. You need to model the right attitude along with your actions.
- Be honest with yourself and your child. Admit when you are wrong, and ask God to show you the correct way. In the process, you will be teaching your son to do the same.
- Remember, don't judge your son when he makes the wrong choice

EXECUTE THE PLAY
INVENTORY YOUR TIME

Moms and dads, answer these questions as honestly as possible. Sometimes what we think and know to be priorities don't actually flesh themselves out in our daily lives. It's good to write down what's important, but then also inventory our actions to see if they match up.

What are the most valuable things in my life?

1.

2.

3.

4.

5.

How do I spend my time, resources, and energy on these priorities?

1.

2.

3.

4.

5.

*Optional

Have a close friend and/or your son answer the same questions about you. Don't show them your answers. After they have finished, compare the lists. Be honest and humble about any discrepancies. The idea here is for you to not only be aware of how you see yourself but to also be aware of how others see you. This isn't a time to explain yourself, just to learn.

EXTRA CREDIT

For the next week, keep a log of what you do. Use the columns below to keep a rough draft of your calendar. Consider using some form of shorthand to make it easier to record your information (F=family; C=church; W=work; etc.). Or you may want to record more detail on a separate sheet of paper where you have more room. If you already know that some of the time slots are full, go ahead and fill them in. But try to carve out time for what's important.

	Sun	Mon	Tues	Wed	Thur	Fri	Sat
7a	—	—	—	—	—	—	—
8a	—	—	—	—	—	—	—
9a	—	—	—	—	—	—	—
10a	—	—	—	—	—	—	—
11a	—	—	—	—	—	—	—
12p	—	—	—	—	—	—	—
1p	—	—	—	—	—	—	—
2p	—	—	—	—	—	—	—
3p	—	—	—	—	—	—	—
4p	—	—	—	—	—	—	—
5p	—	—	—	—	—	—	—
6p	—	—	—	—	—	—	—
7p	—	—	—	—	—	—	—
8p	—	—	—	—	—	—	—
9p	—	—	—	—	—	—	—
10p	—	—	—	—	—	—	—

A =
ASK &
LISTEN

"Mom. Mom. Mom. Mom. Mom."

Growing up, how many times did you try to pester your mom into submission by sheer, repetitive nagging? We've all done it, and if you're a mom, you've likely experienced the willpower of the nagging toddler. It's one thing if your son is just trying to wear you down at the grocery store asking you for the fifteenth time if he can have a soda and a candy bar. But it's another thing if there's truly something on his heart and he needs to tell you.

The greatest need each person has is to be loved. We all want to be loved, and one of the major ways we show others that love is when we truly listen to them. The best way you can show your son how to listen is by listening to God.

Remember, the two-minute drill clock is ticking, and life and family are going to march on. That annoying "Mom" or "Dad" five times in a row may eventually just turn into "Hey." Pretty soon you'll be lucky if you get a text or a phone call.

You have a window of opportunity *now*. The time for action is *now*. It's critical for you to show your son what it looks like to ask and listen to God. That's what a real man does.

HUDDLE UP

REVIEW

■ *Use the following questions to kick off your small-group meeting by discussing what group members learned about themselves when they inventoried their time this past week. Also allow them an opportunity to share other things the Lord has revealed to them about relating to their sons.*

What did you discover about yourself from the "Inventory Your Time" activity?

How do the things you say you value really line up with how you spend your time, resources, and energy?

What surprises did you encounter?

PREVIEW

■ *Use the next few minutes to answer the following questions as a small group. It will help you get the conversation going about what it means to ask God for direction and really listen to Him. Take turns answering the questions as a group until everyone has had a chance to share their thoughts.*

What does it mean when you listen to someone with your ears, eyes, face, and body?

Who in your life has exemplified this best?

VIDEO DISCUSSION

I love sharing the story of Big Oak Ranch. In this video I'm going to be talking about the importance of asking God for direction in life and really listening to Him—even when things are going good. Especially when we get off track, we need Him to show us the road back. Both Brodie and Reagan talk about their journeys back to the ranch and how they had to stop and listen to God. Eathan recounts the first time he really heard God speak to him. These stories, in one way or another, are just a reflection of God's faithfulness to lead us and show us the way. When we look into the Scripture after the video, you will see what Jesus has to say about asking God for daily provision and how we can do the same.

- **Play Video 3: Ask & Listen (11:14)**

- *If your group is large, break into smaller groups of three or four to discuss the next two questions. Encourage group members to write down their personal takeaways as others share insights, stories, struggles, or victories.*

Describe a time when you said, "I got this," when instead you should have said, "God's got this."

Brodie shared that he learned later in life the difference between *hearing* his coach and *listening to* his coach. For you, what's the main difference, consequence, or implication between hearing from God and listening to God?

■ *Bring everyone back together as a large group to continue your discussion.*

Based on what you have already shared with one another about your experiences, what are the obstacles or barriers most common to all of you that keep you from being a man or woman of prayer?

In the video I made the statement that, "There is no wrong way to pray. There is no wrong way to listen. But you have to be willing and available." Parents, this is what lies at the heart of the matter. We have to be willing and available to God and to our sons. We are on this journey together, and I think once you make it a priority and a habit to ask God for wisdom and then wait and listen for the answer, He is going to show you and your sons how big He really is.

SMALL-GROUP DISCUSSION

What's the opposite of being distracted by this world? Being persistent in seeking God. Just like being distracted leads down a destructive path, persistence leads down a powerful path—one surrounded with prayer.

Jesus taught His disciples how to pray. As you read this week's Scripture passage, keep in mind that Jesus is only teaching His disciples what God has already taught Him. This parable about prayer is a lesson that Jesus has already learned. This is coming straight from God the Father.

This week's passage comes from the Gospels. Jesus is teaching on prayer and the value of persistent prayer. **Read Luke 11:1-13**. This is an amazing parable that Jesus tells to His disciples to teach them the value of prayer—not just prayer, but persistent prayer. As you answer the questions below, imagine your son seeing you applying these verses and praying to God on a consistent basis.

> Given what Jesus is communicating in these verses, how are you supposed to model "Ask & Listen" when God either doesn't answer immediately or says "no"?

> Verse 11 specifically addresses a parent's relationship with his or her son, particularly how a parent responds to a legitimate request. "What father among you, if his son asks for a fish, will give him a snake instead of a fish?" What do you think this verse reveals about how you apply the ask and listen principles?

As a parent you actually perform both roles in Jesus' parable—responding to your son's knock and making a request of God. How can this unique paradigm help you teach your son how to ask and listen to God?

GOAL

Jesus understood the value of asking God for direction and listening for His reply. In Scripture we see that Jesus would often find uninterrupted time in the morning to listen to God. But He also listened to people when they needed Him. Constantly people pressed Him and clung to Him. They needed to be healed, or they wanted to hear His teaching. When they had a pressing need, Jesus listened. He learned this from His Heavenly Father because God was always there for Him. As you pursue this principle of persistent prayer, remember that Jesus learned it, too.

> "We cannot teach our children how to listen to God if we're not listening to Him and to them. Children see and can pinpoint the distractions, be it money, power, improper relationships, the worship of sports, TV. You may think they don't know, but they do."
>
> THE TWO-MINUTE DRILL TO MANHOOD

Psalm 32:8, says, "I will instruct you and show you the way to go; with My eye on you, I will give counsel." This Psalm tells us that God keeps His eye on us—always. Not only that, but He is tireless in His availability to us as a counselor.

Obviously God has characteristics that we do not—omnipotence being one, tirelessness being another. How can you take this same promise and apply it to your relationship with your son?

How are you living out Psalm 32:8 in front of your son? As a group, list a few ways this can be modeled within a family.

His Word says that He will be there for us. And the promises of God are true. Proverbs 2:10-12 says,

> "For wisdom will enter your mind,
> and knowledge will delight your heart.
> Discretion will watch over you,
> and understanding will guard you,
> rescuing you from the way of evil."

Where do you go from here? What practical steps is God asking you to take to help your son know what it means to ask God for help and listen for the answer?

Highlights

- Teaching your son how to ask and listen and modeling it are the same thing. You teach it by modeling it.
- Your sons need to see what it looks like when you ask God for help.
- Your son knows what distracts you from them and God. You can't fool them.
- Persistent prayer isn't about what you say, it's about how available you are.

EXECUTE THE PLAY
THE "ASK & LISTEN" FAMILY FORUM

Moms and dads, this activity is about coming together as a family to communicate about significant things as well as modeling an important process for your son.

You heard in the video that early on at the ranch when times were tough, sometimes I would call everyone together so we could pray. I never shared anything that was inappropriate for my family or employees to hear. But I did want them to know, in general terms, that there were some pressing financial demands that needed to be met. We needed to come together as a family and trust God for these things.

You can model this kind of asking and listening with your family on two levels.

Level One

Call an official family forum. Make sure you have an item of concern ready to share before you pull everyone together. It may be a financial need for your family or someone else's family. It may be a relational issue that needs to be addressed— maybe forgiveness and restoration need to be attained. Regardless of the need, keep it age appropriate for your children. Nothing too heavy. The point of sharing is not to scare, frighten, or stress your children to the point of worry or anxiety. They need to be protected from that kind of stress. Find a way to share the need in an age-appropriate way. Once you have shared, pray to God and ask Him for help.

Level Two

After you have asked God to listen to you, turn to your son and ask him if there is something he needs help with. Don't try to force anything out of him. This is just an opportunity you are giving him to share. You are letting him know that you are listening. If he doesn't share anything, that's OK. More times and opportunities will come later. But if he does share a need, take time to listen. Don't try to fix it. And then spend a few minutes in prayer together for that need.

You can do this at a regular, set time for your family or just as needed.

EXTRA CREDIT

Memorize the six stages of getting off course.

1. Distracted

2. Deceived

3. Defeated

4. Discouraged

5. Disillusioned

6. Despair

Spend some time this week identifying specific circumstances and appropriate reactions for stopping the downward spiral. Don't wait until you have fallen all the way down to despair before you turn around. Admit you are off course and ask God to get you back on course with Him.

N=NEVER COMPROMISE

When we think about compromise, many analogies come to mind. When the hull of the Titanic was compromised, it sunk. When the structural integrity of a building is compromised, it collapses. When a tire is punctured, it goes flat. If doctors or nurses compromise the sterile field when entering surgery, they risk bringing infection to the patient. A child's car seat installed incorrectly compromises the baby's safety.

Nothing good comes from the compromise of character, faith, or integrity.

As an athlete who loves the game of football, I know all about the potential dangers of compromise. Games are won and lost on the ability of each player to play his position with the fullest of integrity—without compromise, without breaking.

In football, the line of scrimmage is where every play begins. In life, the line of scrimmage represents the choices you can make every day. Every play is designed to score a touchdown. But if one person doesn't do his or her job, or if one position gets compromised over and over again without correction, the defense will exploit that weakness. There will be no progress. There will be no touchdown celebrations.

Life is the same way. Our boys need to understand the seriousness of compromise, and we need to be the best example of consistency possible. In our pursuit of true M.A.N.H.O.O.D., our response to the temptation to compromise should always be, "Never!"

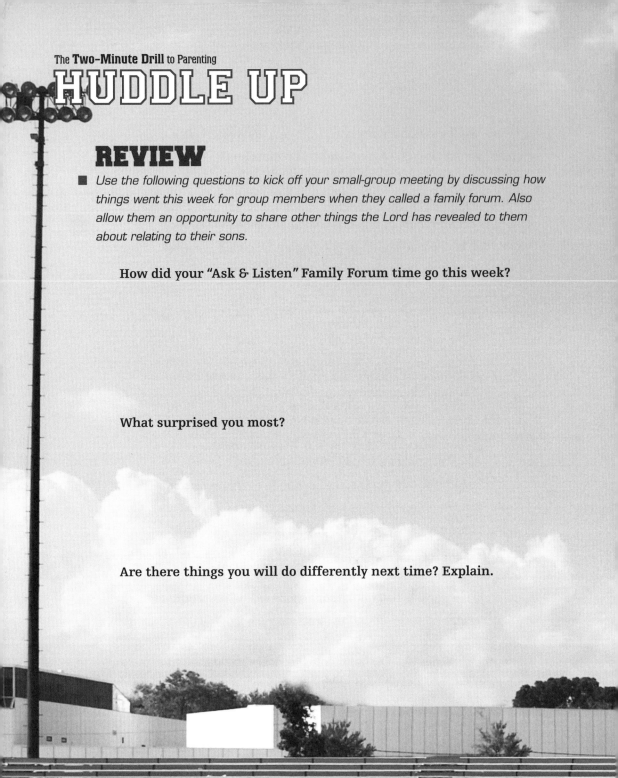

HUDDLE UP

REVIEW

■ *Use the following questions to kick off your small-group meeting by discussing how things went this week for group members when they called a family forum. Also allow them an opportunity to share other things the Lord has revealed to them about relating to their sons.*

How did your "Ask & Listen" Family Forum time go this week?

What surprised you most?

Are there things you will do differently next time? Explain.

The TWO-MINUTE Drill to MANHOOD

LifeWay

PREVIEW

■ *Use the next few minutes to answer the following questions as a small group. It will help you get the conversation going about what it means to never compromise. Take turns answering the questions as a group until everyone has had a chance to share their thoughts.*

As it relates to ethical situations—doing what's right or wrong—compare and contrast flexibility and compromise.

Who in your life has shown the greatest ability to remain flexible without compromising? Explain.

KICKOFF

VIDEO DISCUSSION

I think the thing you will be most aware of after this video is how easy it is for compromise to settle into our lives unnoticed. From TV shows to football games to how we treat our spouse in front of our boys, we make tiny choices that show consistency or compromise. Whether it's living at the ranch and abiding by the "no tobacco" policy or raising our kids to watch what's best on TV, each of us talks a little about our struggle to live a life without compromise.

■ **Play Video 4: Never Compromise (13:21)**

■ *If your group is large, break into smaller groups of three or four to discuss the following question. Encourage group members to write down their personal take-aways as others share insights, stories, struggles, or victories.*

> At the beginning of the video, I shared the story of how Brodie called me out on having my "Fuzz Buster" in the car. When children ask questions that challenge our actions and integrity, what they are really saying is, "This doesn't make sense." In response we need to change our behavior one way or the other. How have you been called out by your kids?

■ *Bring everyone back together as a large group to continue your discussion.*

Compromise is not the end. In fact, it may be just the beginning. In the video you heard, "Compromise just opens up another door to sin or another situation." How have you seen this played out in a specific situation?

As your boys get older, you may be questioned more and more about the consistency of your own actions. If the question starts out with the phrase, "What's the difference between … ," be prepared to listen without pride or bias. Here are several examples.

- "You tell me not to do drugs, but I see you drink too much."
- "You tell me not to steal, but I heard you bragging about cheating on your taxes."
- "You tell me to always tell the truth, but I heard mom lie to cover for you."
- "You tell me to pay attention, but I see you text and drive all the time."

Our sons are processing life through the filter called "Mom and Dad." When they have a question, we need to be honest with our answers. We can turn to God's Word for conviction and correction.

SMALL-GROUP DISCUSSION

The only real, true remedy for compromise and inconsistent actions is to go to God's Word and let it examine us. Once we know the truth, if we will be honest and admit where we don't live up to it, God will help us correct our course. No one is perfect, but that's never been the issue I've stressed in my family or at Big Oak Ranch. The issue is making the necessary changes in your own personal life once you have been confronted with the truth of your actions.

Read Hebrews 4:12. This passage is clear on the role God's Word plays in our lives.

> This passage compares God's Word to a "double-edged" sword. What does this mean and how can you apply it for helping your son avoid the kind of compromise that can cripple?

> As a parent, you need to avoid compromises of character as well. What practices can be put in place for examining your own thoughts and intentions?

> When it comes to Scripture and how it relates to being a mother or father to your son, why do you think it's good for it to be "sharp" and "penetrating"?

What role has God's Word played in the life of your family?
How could it be stronger? Where do you need help?

In the video, Brodie spoke about the time his football coach called him out. "Never play to the potential of your opponent," he said. "Always play to a standard." What a great analogy for our lives with God. We should never look at the world's system (and the Enemy's standards) and lower ourselves to meet them. Instead, we should always be aware that God calls us to live by a higher standard.

GOAL

When you read about the life of Christ, you see at the very beginning of His ministry Jesus was tempted by the Devil (see Matthew 4:1-11). Satan approached Jesus three times and tempted Him to compromise His identity, mission, and trust in God. Three times Jesus replied by quoting Scripture. He met the temptation to compromise with the Word of God that He had hidden in His heart. This is how He fought against the temptations of the Enemy. Moms and dads, your parenting approach should be the same. Use the Word of God like Jesus did. Show them the Scriptures. Help them memorize it. Be intentional to teach your boys the power of God's Word for their everyday lives.

Proverbs 15:31 says, "One who listens to life-giving rebukes will be at home among the wise." When you recognize compromise (or the potential for it) in your son's life, you need to give "life-giving" correction in a firm but loving way.

> **What is the difference between a "life-giving" rebuke and a life-sapping rebuke? Give examples.**

Read 2 Timothy 4:2 for this last set of questions. In his final days, Paul encouraged young Timothy to, "Proclaim the message; persist in it whether convenient or not; rebuke, correct, and encourage with great patience and teaching."

> **In 2 Timothy 4:2, Paul refers to the issue of convenience. How do matters of convenience play into your execution of the two-minute drill where compromise is concerned? Be specific.**

> **Think about your current relationship with your son. In what areas do you need to show more patience or careful instruction as you teach him about compromise?**

One of the best ways to set the tone about making choices is to make it a family decision. When Joshua made a statement about serving the Lord in Joshua 24:15, he declared his allegiance to God for his entire family. "If serving the LORD seems undesirable to you, then choose for yourselves this day whom you will serve. ... But as for me and my household, we will serve the LORD" (Joshua 24:15, NIV).

"We all make choices every day in the different things we do. In those choices we can be flexible, or we can compromise. They look a lot like each other, but they are very different. Flexibility involves being willing to adapt and yield to the point of bending. It doesn't ask for a complete break. Compromise is a willingness to move from a principle to a middle ground, making a complete break. It involves conceding, and to me conceding means losing."

THE TWO-MINUTE DRILL TO MANHOOD

Highlights

- Compromise is not being consistent and following through with something God has asked you to do.
- Compromise can happen anytime and anywhere.
- Prideful parents won't want to admit when they get called out for inconsistency.
- God's Word is powerful and can help develop a consistency in your son's spiritual life.

EXECUTE THE PLAY
HEAD-ON OR AROUND THE BLOCK

I remember explaining to my children why we must meet our personal problems head-on. I used a football analogy and tried to explain it this way: Each football play is designed for the offensive players to block the defensive players in such a way that it creates a seam or a hole through which the running back can carry the ball. Sometimes the running back can't see the seam at first because the play is developing slowly. In this case, the player who's carrying the football is tempted to run "around the block" (the wrong direction because he believes the play isn't working). If he does this, it shows that he is not disciplined enough to execute the play. He needs to follow the design of the play and meet the defenders head-on, even if he can't see a way through. It's tough to do that sometimes. It looks like it would be easier to go around. But that's not the design of the play, and the running back will find himself all alone. We need to be in the right place even in the difficult times and meet our problems like men.

Parents, it's necessary that your child understand what it looks like to make these kinds of choices. Your son needs to see both sides of it—the resolve and regret, the success and failure. This week, recall and reflect on challenging times when you met a problem head-on or when you failed to do so. These will be good stories to share with your son when you talk about never compromising.

Here are some questions for either scenario—head on or around the block.

Meeting a problem "head-on" and not compromising:

Describe the situation. What were the choices in front of you?

What variables or factors were present that tempted you to go "around the block" and take the easy way out?

What specific choice did you make? Identify the decision that allowed you to not compromise.

What would have been the costs of compromise? What lessons did you learn through the experience?

Avoiding a problem and finding a way to compromise:

Describe the situation. What were the choices in front of you?

What variables or factors were present that tempted you to go "around the block" and take the easy way out?

What specific choice did you make? Identify the moment of compromise that followed.

What were the costs of this compromise? What lessons did you learn through the experience?

H =

HANDLE
YOUR
BUSINESS

Everything we have talked about so far assumes two things: (1) that you have a solid relationship with God, and (2) that you are pursuing an authentic relationship with your son. These beams form the cross for teaching your son about true manhood. You have to pick it up daily, be intentional, and follow through for it to work.

When you begin teaching your son about handling his business, things can quickly get real. This is where the rubber meets the road. For this lesson to truly take root in the heart of your son, from time to time you will need to withhold some things from him. And sometimes that isn't easy for us. Our natural tendency as parents is to want to give our kids everything we didn't have as children—and more. Let's face it, no parent wants to see his or her son do without. But when we let our sons do without now, the trade off is worth it in the long run.

At the ranch, *work* is not a four-letter word. Actually, it's just the opposite. When we work hard at the ranch, that's when the boys see their "dads" at their best. Chores give us an excuse to spend time with our sons—especially chores that need to be taught or explained or require more than one person to accomplish. This is probably one of the most practical ways you can be present in your son's life, and it gives you the means through which to teach him how to handle business.

The Two-Minute Drill to Parenting

HUDDLE UP

REVIEW

■ *Use the following questions to kick off your small-group meeting by discussing how things went this week for group members. Allow them an opportunity to debrief about the "Head-On or Around the Block" activity as well as to share other things the Lord has revealed to them about relating to their sons.*

Were you able to come up with at least one story of a time when you met a problem head on? How about a time when you failed to do so?

Briefly share one story with the group and be prepared to receive suggestions from other group members of how your story could be used to teach your son about never compromising. Be willing to offer suggestions to others in the group as they share their stories as well.

PREVIEW

■ *Use the next few minutes to answer the following questions as a small group. It will help you get the conversation going about what it means to handle your business. Take turns answering the questions as a group until everyone has had a chance to share their thoughts.*

What event helped you realize that growing up meant more freedom as well as more *responsibility*?

What specific circumstances helped you see the road to responsibility most clearly? Who taught you the most about this—your first boss, parent, teacher, family friend?

KICKOFF

VIDEO DISCUSSION

Throughout this video segment you'll hear me describe the five things I think are non-negotiable when it comes to handling your business. With decades on the ranch watching these boys grow up, I have pretty much seen it all. I know what the end goal is for these young men, and I have seen what it takes to get them there. I've also seen what can get in the way. Reagan, Brodie, and the boys from the ranch all have their stories to tell. From chores to allowances to earning privileges, all of the experiences you'll hear have given these boys a chance at real manhood. And as you will find out in the group time, even the smallest details matter. It's the little things that add up.

■ **Play Video 5: Handle Your Business (13:20)**

■ *If your group is large, break into smaller groups of three or four to discuss the following question. Encourage group members to write down their personal takeaways as others share insights, stories, struggles, or victories.*

> I talked about the five areas of handling your business. Which have you already been implementing? Which have you avoided? Explain.

■ *Bring everyone back together as a large group to continue your discussion.*

> You could see it in his eyes. Eathan was proud of that car he purchased after six months of flipping burgers. Talk about the opportunities you are affording your boys by not giving them a car (or other possession) they want. What is the payoff?

One of Reagan's childhood memories was always having to do chores. She'd have to clean the horse stables before she could ride the horses. This taught her the importance of getting her business done first, then she could pursue pleasure. How are you teaching your son this lesson?

What are the common obstacles (personal, cultural) that get in the way of that?

Parents, there's a big difference between trying to prepare your son for the way and trying to prepare the way for your son. We think we can prepare the way, but that's like thinking we can change the world to fit our boys. That's just foolish. Like we learned in Session 1, the godless culture of this world will always be there bringing difficult circumstances and temptations on its own. It will always be there to challenge your son's character, morals, and ability to thrive and be successful. It's the tough decisions—like not giving them everything they want—that will help them understand what it feels like to persevere and earn it. It's tough to do, but it's the right thing.

SMALL-GROUP DISCUSSION

When you read some of the stories in the Bible, it's natural to wonder, *Whoa! Did that really happen?* There's one such story found in Leviticus 10 about two brothers. Nadab and Abihu were the sons of Aaron, the brother of Moses. Aaron was the first priest in the Old Testament, and he was responsible for all the worship, sacrifices, and tabernacle ceremonies. God had given specific instructions on how to go about doing all of this. He left nothing to chance.

Read Leviticus 10:1-11. I bet Aaron wished he'd taught his boys to handle their business better. Especially since their business was representing God to the nation of Israel.

> **Reading this passage through the lens of handling your business, what seems to be Aaron's biggest mistake as a parent?**

> **What do you think this passage says regarding what God thinks about knowing the details and handling your business?**

The sooner we teach our boys about true manhood, the better off they will be. What are some practical ways you can stress the value and importance of these five manhood principles?

What changes can you make even now to communicate and teach these things to your son?

GOAL

Parents who expect their sons to handle their business are really stealing a page from Jesus' life with His disciples. Honesty, integrity, making wise financial decisions, working hard, living a moral life—all of these principles are found in God and His kingdom. But there's got to be an intentionality on our part as parents to point our boys in the right direction. Jesus was constantly teaching His disciples to count the cost. Luke 14 shows us the true cost to be a disciple. As parents, we need to constantly teach our boys to count the cost. Because it does cost something to be a real man and enter into manhood.

You've heard the old expression that the devil is in the details, right? Well, God's in the details, too. He wants us to pay attention to the details as we teach our boys to handle their business. What are some of the details that God has brought to your attention for you to address?

It is estimated that 85 percent of a child's character is determined by the time he or she is six years old. None of us want to produce a selfish child. Therefore, training our children in the art of sharing with others at an early age is a must. It is a standard life lesson that we cannot let slip away because the older they get, the harder the lesson will be to teach."

THE TWO-MINUTE DRILL TO MANHOOD

How do you model a work ethic that results not in acquiring more stuff but rather in blessing others? How can you be better?

What would a boy who is soon to be a man miss if you failed to instill a giver's heart in him?

What are some practical lessons we can live out with our sons to help them develop a giver's heart?

A 5-year-old doing little chores, a 10-year-old helping Dad mow the lawn, a 16-year-old getting a job to pay for his car, a 20-year-old taking a full load in college, and a 25-year-old in business for himself—they are all experiencing the same amount of stress or challenge in life. It's all relative to what they are able to handle. And that's the point. First Corinthians 10:13 says, "No temptation has overtaken you except what is common to humanity. God is faithful, and He will not allow you to be tempted beyond what you are able, but with the temptation He will also provide a way of escape so that you are able to bear it." So when your boy is tempted to bail out on his responsibilities as a man, with God's help, he will be able to withstand it.

Highlights

- Your work ethic (witnessed by your son) sets the tone for everything else.
- Your son will learn time management by watching you manage your time.
- Start by giving your son the opportunity to manage his money on a small scale.
- Don't prepare the way for your son. Instead, prepare your son for the way.
- Sometimes allowing your son to earn something is better than just giving it to him.

EXECUTE THE PLAY
BUDGETING FOR A GOAL

Moms and dads, here are a couple of helpful activities for you to do with your sons related to helping them learn how to handle money responsibly.

Start with an item your son wants to purchase (computer, video game, iPad®, concert tickets, even a car) and create a budget that sets weekly or monthly benchmarks for saving. Use the space below for notes. Show him that through saving money his goal is attainable. Project how much the item will cost and estimate how much he can earn each week or month in pursuit of that item. You can do this for any age. (If you don't give your younger son an allowance, now would be a good time to begin. Boys can learn money management and consequences for bad decisions through how they handle an allowance.)

If your son is of working age, set up a mock interview. Ask him to prepare, dress, and groom himself appropriately. Pretending you are the employer, ask him three or four of these questions:

- Describe some of the responsibilities you have had at home or in your previous job.

- What major challenges or problems have you faced? How did you handle them?

- What have you learned from your mistakes?

- Which job (or chore) has been the most rewarding? Least rewarding? Explain.

- What makes you different from all the other young men who are applying for this job?

- Why should I hire you?

When you are finished, talk about how it went. Ask him these questions:

- What went right?

- What went wrong?

- Where do you feel most confident in your answers?

- Where do you feel you could most improve?

O-ONE
PURPOSE

Coaches and parents have a lot in common.

Good coaches know their players as well as parents know their children. Coaches have the responsibility to come up with the game plan. In the same way, God has given parents the responsibility to provide their kids with a plan to succeed. A lot of times, good coaches will take the blame when their team performs poorly on the field. Sadly enough, good parents often get blamed when their kids find trouble and misadventure.

Good coaches will go the extra mile to ensure their players are taken care of—ice packs, heating tubs, wrapping ankles, bandaging bruised ribs. Parents are no different. They spend countless hours working hard to provide the best for their kids. They are concerned when their children are hurt by friends or schoolmates. They would put a bandage on their souls if it would make them feel better.

Coaches and parents both are focused on one thing, one purpose—preparing for victory. Coaches want their team to win the game. We do all we can to prepare our boys to win in life. This is what parenting with purpose is all about. I invite you to live out your purpose and showcase it to your sons. Let them see you pursue God and His purpose for your life.

HUDDLE UP

REVIEW

■ *Use the following questions to kick off your small-group meeting by discussing how things went this week for group members. Allow them an opportunity to debrief about the "Budgeting for a Goal" activity as well as to share other things the Lord has revealed to them about relating to their sons.*

What item or activity does your son want to save for?

What difference do you think it made in your son's thinking as you created a budget and set benchmarks, showing him that through hard work and discipline his goal is attainable?

If you had a mock interview, how did it go? What new things did you and your son learn from this exercise?

The
TWO-
MINUTE Drill
to MANHOOD

✦LifeWay

PREVIEW

■ *Use the next few minutes to answer the following questions as a small group. It will help you get the conversation going about what it means to live with one purpose. Take turns answering the questions as a group until everyone has had a chance to share their thoughts.*

Discuss the purpose of the following activities, clubs, and organizations.

- Civic organization
- Youth sports leagues
- Academic clubs
- Scouting
- Music/instrumental training
- High school sports

Compare the coach and player for a moment. How much responsibility do each have in winning or losing the game?

In what ways do the coach and player work together to be successful at winning?

Big Oak Ranch

KICKOFF

VIDEO DISCUSSION

In this video you're going to hear us speak about finding our purpose in God and what that looks like. I'll be discussing how pleasing God and obeying God relates to finding your purpose in Him. Tee talks about living your purpose and walking with God in front of your kids. Reagan recalls how contagious that was—seeing and watching her parents pursue God and never look back. It's important to do this now and bring that expectation to your boys. Talk about God all the time and include Him in your conversation on every level. As you focus on the following discussion starters, let our testimony bring some depth to the conversation.

■ **Play Video 6: One Purpose (13:40)**

■ *If your group is large, break into smaller groups of three or four to discuss the following questions. Encourage group members to write down their personal takeaways as others share insights, stories, struggles, or victories.*

> **Talk about the different purposes you pursued when you were younger. Which brought you closer to God? Which took you further from God?**

> **Who helped you discover your purpose in life? Talk about their sphere of influence over you. What made them so special?**

■ *Bring everyone back together as a large group to continue your discussion.*

> **When it comes to finding purpose in life, parents should be the best coaches for their sons. What measures are you taking to coach your son into his purpose in life—spiritually and vocationally? What steps do you need to take to move from the sidelines to the field?**

At this point in the game, you as a parent really need to take on the role of coach. Like a coach, you need to exemplify a commanding presence on the "practice field." This can be tough to do, especially if you aren't living God's purpose for your life in front of your son. Moms and dads, your home is the practice field for life for your sons. Take command of it.

SMALL-GROUP DISCUSSION

As parents, we cannot underestimate the impact we have on our sons. The sphere of influence we have over them is a result of God saying, "These boys are yours. You'll have them for a while, and it's your job to give them back to me." That's why it's important that our lives match up with God's purpose and His Word. The Bible reveals some of the deepest truths about who we are and who we're supposed to be. It showcases humanity in every circumstance—the human condition with and without God.

We are going to look at several passages of Scripture today. These verses reveal the desire of man's heart to find and know God.

> Read Psalm 84:10. In this passage David expresses his desire to be with God and experience Him. How do you express this kind of desire in front of your family—verbally, emotionally, intellectually, physically?

> What does Psalm 84:10 reveal to you about purpose—both for you and the way you might coach your son in the area of purpose?

> Read Ephesians 2:10 and Psalm 139:14. Both Paul and the psalmist recognize the value God places on us as His most wonderful creation. Look for the key phrases in these verses. How can you use these Scriptures to foster a sense of purpose in your son?

In the video message you heard Eathan mention what he has learned about finding purpose in God from his "mom and dad" at the ranch. Unfortunately, he didn't have these kinds of godly role models in his birth family. Before Big Oak Ranch, his journey to manhood was on a very different path. Because of that, he now has two very distinct perspectives when joy or heartache come his way—one with Christ and one without Christ.

Read Philippians 3:7-11. This verse is about surrender. Many times the first step toward discovering ultimate and final purpose is letting go of something and surrendering to God. How can you model—or how have you modeled—surrender for your son?

GOAL

When Jesus completed His work on the cross, His purpose in eternity was complete. Following His Father's plan, Jesus laid down His life for the sin of the world. In the Book of Colossians, Paul talks about how Jesus Christ paves the way back to God—calling us to find our purpose in Him. "All the broken and dislocated pieces of the universe—people and things, animals and atoms—get properly fixed and fit together in vibrant harmonies, all because of his death, his blood that poured down from the cross" (Colossians 1:19-20, MSG). What an awesome promise from God. No matter how broken and busted we are, all who find Christ get put back together because of His death on the cross.

> As parents, we need a clear, tenacious focus
> on who we want our children to be. I'm not
> talking about what we want our children to
> *do* but who we want our children to *be*. We
> need to be prepared and have everything
> rock solid in our heads so that we can
> anticipate where they will be on that field.
>
> THE TWO-MINUTE DRILL TO MANHOOD

If your son knows who he is in Christ, then he has a solid foundation. But he also needs to see that his vocation has a purpose in Christ. In what ways can you, as his parent, show that your vocation is sacred and has a place in God's purpose?

How have you coached your son in the areas of professional pursuits and ambition?

What have you learned about these pursuits?

Parents, our function in life is to prepare our sons for life—to train, lead, and guide them. We need to inspire them as well. That's what great coaches do. They inspire players to be the best they can be. They motivate them and point them in the right direction. They recognize strengths and weaknesses in their players and refuse to give up until they have reached their full potential. When they see the best, coaches exploit it for good and push their players as far as they can go without burnout. It's a delicate balance between coach and player.

Highlights

- We want to shape who our children are going to be, not what we want them to do.
- We need to be honest about their talents and abilities but give them freedom to pursue a vocation or life's calling.
- We should model obedience to God and expect the same from our sons.
- The highest goal of a parent is to introduce his or her children

EXECUTE THE PLAY
DO YOU REALLY KNOW?

It's one thing to know *about* someone, and it's another thing to actually *know* him or her. This exercise will help you communicate two things: (1) that you really want to know your son, and (2) that you desire he know Jesus Christ on a personal level.

Use the following questions as discussion starters with your son. They will help him better understand purpose as well as help you both better *know* him:

- What is your favorite moment in the Bible?

- What do you enjoying doing most?

- What do you enjoy talking about most?

- Who do you admire?

- If money were no object, what would you want to do?

- What is your favorite subject to study? Why?

- What stops you when you're flipping channels? Why?

- What can we do together that you would enjoy?

The application here is a relational one, and this activity can help you launch a meaningful discussion. We need to do more than just read about someone or memorize facts to really know him or her. We know someone when we spend time together.

It's the same with Jesus. We can read about Him, memorize facts about Him, talk about Him, go to church to learn about Him, but unless we believe in Jesus and spend time with Him, we will not *know* Him.

Finish up this discussion with your son by looking at these two passages together and talking about what these verses tell us about who we are and who God is.

I will praise You because I have been remarkably
and wonderfully made. Your works are
wonderful, and I know this very well.
PSALM 139:14

For we are His creation, created in Christ Jesus for good works,
which God prepared ahead of time so that we should walk in them.
EPHESIANS 2:10

0-ONE
BODY

The problem with looking to the culture for truth is that it's always shifting and changing. Fads come and go, but even if a cultural trend stays the same, there's always going to be a reaction to it—creating a sort of counter-cultural option. Sometimes these are good, and sometimes they aren't.

Consider the hedonistic culture of ancient Greece. They celebrated the athlete and the body so much that the Olympian athletes would compete totally naked! Wow, no thanks! But many early Christians countered this culture and swung all the way over to the other side. They refused themselves any kind of worldly enjoyment and denied themselves any pleasure at all because they thought the "flesh" was evil. They were living a disciplined life, but they were doing it for the wrong reason.

Worldly culture may lie about our bodies, but parents, if we respond in some knee-jerk fashion, we may find ourselves in error in a different way. More importantly, we may find ourselves in a different kind of conflict with our sons.

That's why in this session we are going to look at this aspect of true M.A.N.H.O.O.D., share what we've learned over the years at Big Oak Ranch, and learn from God's Word. As your son begins to physically mature, it's crucial he get a well-rounded, biblical view of his body. He needs to feel comfortable in his own skin and understand why God created him.

HUDDLE UP

REVIEW

■ *Use the following questions to kick off your small-group meeting by discussing how things went this week for group members. Allow them an opportunity to debrief about the "Do You Really Know?" activity as well as to share other things the Lord has revealed to them about relating to their sons.*

What new things did you learn about your son through this activity?

Were there things he learned about himself? About God? Explain.

What next steps do you plan to take to help your son continue to get to *know* Jesus Christ on a personal level?

PREVIEW

■ *Use the next few minutes to answer the following questions as a small group. It will help you get the conversation going about what it means to choose wisely concerning our bodies. Take turns answering the questions as a group until everyone has had a chance to share their thoughts.*

From the Miss America pageant to the Mr. Universe competition, we are a self-saturated, body-conscience culture. On a scale of 1 to 10, how much were you taught growing up about what it means to have a healthy view of your own body?

1   5   10

very little   a lot

What sources seem to be having the most impact on your son related to this body-conscious mindset (i.e., Hollywood, movies, professional sports, friends, fashion, reality TV)?

KICKOFF

VIDEO DISCUSSION

This session you're going to get a glimpse into what it means to take care of your body, because your sons are watching you. Throughout the video I'll talk about how to take care of your body without worshiping it. But I'll also discuss how we show proper respect for girls and their bodies. My son, Brodie, talks about how the temptation for athletes to abuse drugs to get bigger and faster starts in high school. You will hear Reagan share what she's already learning from her little son about visual images on TV. As we move into the heart of this group experience, I hope you will begin to better understand and feel equipped to communicate to your son that our bodies are something we should respect and cherish.

■ **Play Video 7: One Body (10:31)**

■ *If your group is large, break into smaller groups of three or four to discuss the following questions. Encourage group members to write down their personal takeaways as others share insights, stories, struggles, or victories.*

> **Throughout the video I talk about the need to respect what God has given us in our physical bodies. How do you show respect for your body (or your spouse's body) in front of your son?**

> **Because of the sensory overload in this digital age, we as parents have to be vigilant and constantly paying attention to how our family consumes the culture around us. In what ways you have participated in this body-conscience culture and then realized it later?**

■ *Bring everyone back together as a large group to continue your discussion.*

Think about Brodie and Reagan and their testimony during the video segment. Is there a specific issue related to taking care of his body that you don't feel prepared to talk with your son about? If so, why?

The great thing about raising boys is that they eventually become men. Everything you are experiencing will pass. Sometimes you're on offense and sometimes you're on defense. I just don't want you to get discouraged. If you find yourself feeling a little pressed down, recognize it for what it is. Know that you're on defense right now, but it will pass. You will get to play another series. That's why you huddle up with other parents for support and learning. With God's help and you pressing forward, be confident that you are doing the very best job you can.

SMALL-GROUP DISCUSSION

Corinth was a Roman city that was pretty well off. Many of their problems came from their wealth, and apparently they were indulging in a lifestyle that brought more pleasure to themselves than glory to God. Even though the Christ followers had the body-conscious Roman culture to contend with, Paul writes 1 Corinthians with a tone that communicates they should know better. What's the bottom line? Our bodies are a gift given *by* God to be used *for* God.

Read **1 Corinthians 6:19-20** from several translations. How much clearer can it be? Parents, this is probably the most definitive passage of Scripture that speaks directly to the topic of how we are to treat our bodies.

> **Verse 19 says, "Your body is a sanctuary of the Holy Spirit." So, by translation, whatever you're doing with/to your body you're also doing to the Holy Spirit. In what ways does this change how you see your "one body"?**

> **How can you apply the truth of 1 Corinthians 6:19-20 to how you lead your son?**

> **What words or phrases best describe the difference between an owner and a steward?**

How do you exemplify to your son that you are a good steward of what God has given you in your physical body rather than the owner of your body?

GOAL

Jesus recognized that His body was given for a specific purpose. In Hebrews 10:5,8, Jesus says to God, "You prepared a body for Me. I have come to do Your will, God!" Just before His death, on the night of the Passover, Jesus met with His disciples for supper. Luke records that Jesus took the bread and made a symbol for His body. "He took bread, gave thanks, broke it, gave it to them, and said, 'This is My body, which is given for you. Do this in remembrance of Me.'" (Luke 22:19). If Jesus, the very Son of God, recognized that His body had a purpose and surrendered it to the will of God, then how much more should we?

"Taking care of the body given to us by God
includes getting appropriate amounts of sleep;
eating healthy, balanced meals and snacks;
respecting the role of drugs as something to
help combat illness and return us to good
health; and exercising as a way to strengthen
and maintain muscles and joints. Everything
should be done in moderation. The goal should
be to take care of the body, taking care of who
you are, not striving for an unrealistic goal
of being what others say you ought to be."

THE TWO-MINUTE DRILL TO MANHOOD

There are many different aspects of taking care of our bodies
that will need to be addressed as your son continues into
manhood—body shape and image, health and nutrition, sex and
early dating relationships, and self-worth. Take a moment to
discuss some practical ways you can continue to model a godly
example in front of your son and create natural conversations
with your son about these issues:

• how he looks versus who he is

• nutrition and exercise for healthy living

• dating relationships and how he views the opposite sex

The goal to take care of our bodies is a means to an even greater end—to be used by God with maximum capacity. Think about the wasted life who could not serve God or perform at a manageable pace because of drug or alcohol abuse. What about those whose desire and hearts are in the right place, but they have failed to maintain a healthy diet? As a result, they are overweight and have developed easily preventable diseases. Don't underestimate the message you send your son when it comes to your own body.

Highlights

- You cannot depend on cultural trends—no matter how popular— to bring wisdom to your family.
- We are given our bodies for a specific purpose—to use them for God and His purposes.
- There is a big difference between ownership and stewardship when it comes to your body, and you can teach your son the difference.
- When you treat your body with respect, your son will learn to treat his body with respect.

EXECUTE THE PLAY
TAKING CARE TO TAKE CARE

Moms and dads, here are a couple of activities to complete before your next group meeting. There's something here for both younger sons and older sons.

For younger sons:

The greatest way to show your son how to care for his body is to take care of yours. And you can ask your son to help you accomplish this through the following activities:

Tell your son that you are going to let him decide how the two of you play together for 20 minutes a day at least three times a week. Whether this activity is tetherball, basketball, soccer, four-square, etc., this will get him engaged with you. And you will get some exercise as well. But make it about him and what he wants to do. Stay active.

Work together as a team with your son and pick one unhealthy snack or drink to give up during the week. You will both commit to not eating or drinking whatever you have chosen, but then reward yourself on Saturday or Sunday. Do one of these at a time, and let the new habits begin.

For older sons:

Ask your son to name 7 or 8 characteristics of a king and queen.
Next talk about how these attributes translate to real life.
Say something like, "We are all kings and queens in God's eyes.
He makes us special and even calls us co-heirs with Jesus
(see Romans 8:14-17)—the King of kings. God even says that we
are a 'royal' priesthood, set apart for Him (see 1 Peter 2:9).
So, He places immense value on us."

Ask your son, "If you saw every girl as a queen, (because one day
she will be someone's queen), how would that change the way
you treat her? How would that change the way you look at or
view her? How would that change the way you talk about her?"

End the conversation with this thought. "Jesus is our King. He gave His life for
the Church, His bride. He treats her with respect and love. Ephesians 5:25 says,
'Husbands, love your wives, just as Christ loved the church and gave Himself for her.'"

D=
DON'T EVER,
EVER, EVER
GIVE UP

"Don't quit on me!"

I'm pretty sure you've said this out loud to yourself or to someone else.

Maybe you're driving down the road in a old car that's barely making it. Maybe you're a desperate husband or wife pleading with your spouse to save your marriage. Maybe you're a little league coach and your team hasn't won a game.

There's just hope and comfort in knowing that regardless of the circumstances around you, the people you love most will not quit. If you listen to the heartbeat of your son, this is what you would be hearing, too. Impressionable boys need an oak in their lives ... a big oak. And I'm not talking about the ranch this time. I'm speaking directly about you, Mom and Dad. Your son needs to know two things—that you are trusting in a God who will never quit on your family and that you are leading and loving your family in the same way.

This last session is about understanding the influence you have over your son. Don't underestimate the trajectory upon which you put your boy when you respond to adversity with "I'm committed" instead of "I quit." True M.A.N.H.O.O.D. isn't complete until this lesson is learned. Thanks for hanging in there.

Don't quit on me!

The Two-Minute Drill to Parenting

HUDDLE UP

REVIEW

■ *Use the following questions to kick off your small-group meeting by discussing how things went this week for group members. Allow them an opportunity to debrief about the "Taking Care to Take Care" activity as well as to share other things the Lord has revealed to them about relating to their sons.*

In what ways has your son made you more active?

If you have a younger son, what activities did you participate in together? What food or beverage did you give up and how did it go?

If you have an older son, what would you say was the greatest takeaway from your "king and queen" conversation?

PREVIEW

■ *Use the next few minutes to answer the following questions as a small group.*
It will help you get the conversation going about what it means to never give up.
Take turns answering the questions as a group until everyone has had a chance
to share their thoughts.

Talk about your favorite movie (or movie character) that
embodies the idea of never giving up. For example:

• *Facing the Giants*
• the girl in *Soul Surfer*
• *Glory Road*
• the player in *Remember the Titans*
• Rudy in *Rudy*
• Other: _____

Which of the following do you think *most* motivates people to
keep persevering, driving them to never give up? Which one
most motivates you?

• Support system
• Personal discipline
• Desperate situation
• Trying to prove something to themselves
• Trying to prove something to others
• Personal faith in God

LifeWay

Big Oak Ranch

VIDEO DISCUSSION

When you think about it, Big Oak Ranch exists because parents quit on their kids. In this final video message, you're going to hear me talk about what it takes to be the kind of parent—regardless of the circumstances—who refuses to quit. We teach our boys never to give up on anything, as you will hear from more than one of them. My son talks about how the boys at the ranch inspired him to keep playing football despite all the injuries. My wife, Tee, talks about the importance of remaining consistent in our parenting, especially when we're worn out. I'll conclude with some of the most inspiring stories and lessons I've learned from the ranch. All of this discussion is meant to point to a God who refuses to quit on His children.

■ **Play Video 8: Don't Ever, Ever, Ever Give Up (13:49)**

■ *If your group is large, break into smaller groups of three or four to discuss the following questions. Encourage group members to write down their personal takeaways as others share insights, stories, struggles, or victories.*

What life lessons about never giving up do you feel you missed out on growing up? Which ones do you want to make sure your son experiences?

Tee spoke about parenting even when we experience tired moments. What are the "tired moments" for you? What drains you most and threatens to keep you from parenting with intention and clarity?

■ *Bring everyone back together as a large group to continue your discussion.*

> **Think about what Brodie shared and how the boys at the ranch were always in the back of his mind. To a certain degree, they inspired him to not quit football through all the injuries. How much is your son in the back of your mind when it comes to parenting with intentionality? Where have you dropped the ball or let things slide in your relationship?**

God is the ultimate parent. He is the one who refuses to give up. He created us to be with Him, and when we choose to disobey, He pursues us. God has always had a plan to be with His children. When you think about it, the Bible is a big collection of stories about a God who never gives up on His kids. There aren't many good parenting stories in the Bible, but throughout the entire Bible we see God modeling parenthood with His children. This session will take this perspective as we look at the Scripture. We want to learn how to be the kind of parents who continue to pursue their sons as God continues to pursue us.

SMALL-GROUP DISCUSSION

In the game of football, you may find yourself the subject of the "highlight reel" when you make an awesome play. I love the highlight video because you get to relive those moments over and over again.

Highlights are meant to tell the story of the game in snapshots—the pivotal points of the game or where an important play was made. To a certain degree, that's what the Book of Deuteronomy is for the nation of Israel—a big book of highlights. Moses is about to exit the scene. He's been leading Israel around in the desert for 40 years, but Joshua will be leading soon. So what does Moses do? He writes this last book, and he hits the highlights.

Moses knows that the most important thing is to be committed to God because He has made a promise to remain faithful to them. Moses has witnessed God's faithfulness firsthand, and he is confident that God will remain faithful to His children.

Read Deuteronomy 6:4-9. If you want to know the bottom line of what life's all about, look no further.

> God's covenant love for His children is unconditional. This is why Moses commanded them to love God and be committed to Him first. Discuss the different ways you can love your son without condition.

> What does Deuteronomy 6:4-9 have to say about never giving up?

How does Moses include the next generation in this commitment to God?

Translate that into our world. How can we do the same?

GOAL

Jesus reflects the heart of His Father as He lives His life here on earth, and He shows us what it means not to quit. Remember when the Enemy tempted Jesus in the wilderness (see Luke 4:1-13)? Satan wanted Him to give up on His mission, give up on God, give up on humanity, give up on everything. But He stayed the course and learned obedience to the Father. The Gospels tell the story of Jesus' last week leading up to His crucifixion. The crowds loved Him, but the religious elite hated Him. Betrayal was in the air as one of His own, Judas Iscariot, chose to quit on his Rabbi. Soldiers mobbed and beat Him. The crowds chanted "Crucify Him!" The Roman government killed Him. Through all of this, Jesus remained true to His calling. Jesus never quit on God, and He never quits on us. Jesus persevered and endured the cross to the very end (see Philippians 2:1-11).

We are taking on the role of our Heavenly Father when we remain committed parents. List and discuss at least three ways you can show commitment to your son on a daily basis.

> You may be the product of a mom or a dad who let go. Perhaps they let go of their marriage, their own integrity, or their own children. ... As parents, we need to take a close look at our own lives to identify those experiences and influences that make us who we are and what we pass on to our own children. The hardest part is to look and realize that we have a choice to pass character traits on to them or not.
>
> THE TWO-MINUTE DRILL TO MANHOOD

Throughout this entire study we've stressed that you cannot separate your surrendered relationship with God (and how you live it out) from your influential relationship with your son. One directly affects the other. How have you let God heal, correct, or make right the pain of the past so you don't make the same mistakes with your son?

What areas of your life do you need to readdress and recommit so you can exemplify a "don't quit" attitude (i.e., relationships, home project, job, education, etc.)?

Whether you are married, divorced, remarried, single again, or parenting all by yourself, remember this word of encouragement: when you do what's right by your son and you continue to pursue him—regardless of his ability to see you for who you are trying to be—there will be a time in his life when he will realize just how much you stuck with it and made the choice to never, ever give up on him.

Highlights

- Your son needs to see your faithfulness to God on display.
- Parents give their boys a very valuable character trait by teaching them that commitment is a choice, and so is giving up.
- When you choose to never give up on your son, you are modeling who God is to him as well.
- Your son needs to hear you praise and acknowledge his steps toward manhood. It will only encourage him to take bigger steps in

EXECUTE THE PLAY
STICK TO IT

Moms and dads, here's something you can do as a follow-up to your last week of study.

Think of an age-appropriate activity that will necessitate a long-term commitment. Consider the following:

- Plant a small garden (or potted garden plants) and grow some vegetables. Be sure to involve your son in the maintenance.

- Start collecting a series of coins, baseball cards, model cars, etc. that can be given to another person for birthday or Christmas.

- Design the ideal tree house, and then build a miniature version of it with wooden tongue depressors.

- Partner with your son in prayer about a long-term concern that he will understand—maybe the annual standardize testing at school for him and/or a project at work or home for you. Every week or so, talk about the challenges you are currently facing, then make the determination to stick with it, do your best, and not give up.

The point is to bring into focus the idea that some things take a long time to accomplish. This project needs to be long enough to communicate this idea to your son without exhausting you both in the process. Throughout the progress of this activity and even at the conclusion of it, talk about how it felt to want to quit or give up. Then talk about how God never has given up on us.

TWO-MINUTE DRILL

RETREAT PLANS

The following Retreat Plans have been included for parents
and/or groups that would prefer a more intensive study
of *The Two-Minute Drill to Parenting* over a shorter period
of time. For these groups I've put together plans that
include an outline, group discussion questions, and parents
activities adapted or pulled from the Bible study content.
Each session in these retreat plans can be completed in
no more than two hours. Additionally you'll find Parent/
Son activities for those parents who might prefer to take
The Two-Minute Drill to Parenting content and apply it more
directly with one-on-one conversations with their sons.

Included here are the teaching outlines and the parents
activities. You will find the group discussion questions
and parent/son activities on the DVD-ROM included
in the *The Two-Minute Drill to Parenting Leader Kit*
(item 005558745).

RETREAT SESSION 1

Sessions 1–2

THE GAME PLAN // 𝕄 = MASTER

Teaching Outline:
Scriptures: 2 Timothy 3:1-5; 2 Timothy 3:10-17; Matthew 6:24; Romans 6:11-14

I. Preparing ours son for manhood means launching them into the real world
(2 Timothy 3:1-5).

   A. The reality our sons will experience from the world is godless (2 Timothy 3:1-5).

   B. The relationship our sons have with us will ground them (2 Timothy 3:10-17).

II. True manhood begins with choosing the right Master (Matthew 6:24).

   A. Parents should model this motto every day (Romans 6:11-12).

   B. Sons should see their parents surrender to Him in every way
(Romans 6:13-14).

Video Introduction:
You will view two video sessions back-to-back for each retreat session. For retreat
session 1, you will view videos for sessions 1 and 2 on the DVD-ROM.

- Play Video 1 — The Game Plan (10:53)
- Play Video 2 — M = Master (11:09)

Parents Activity:
When the whole M.A.N.H.O.O.D. concept was taking shape, I was planning a
"transition trip" with my son, Brodie. I wanted a special time where I could talk to
him, one-on-one, about what it means to be a man. And God provided a way for
us to go to Alaska on my shoestring budget. This was a great experience. Not
just the destination itself, but the entire journey—how we got there and what we
experienced together.

Complete this worksheet as your parents activity. It will guide you through the logistics of planning such a trip. Fill in each area as best you can. Sharing your ideas and listening to the wisdom of others will help you as well.

What is your objective for the trip?

What are some possible/potential destinations?

    Local Options:

    Intermediate Options (drivable distance—up to 500 miles):

    Extensive Options (requiring air travel):

What is a realistic budget?

- **Travel**

    Gas

    Airfare

    Hotel

    Food

- **Entertainment**

    Gear

    Excursions

    Reservations

    Guides

Use the space below to fill in some key thoughts or ideas that you would like to communicate to your son on your transition trip.

- Master

- Ask & Listen

- Never Compromise

- Handle Your Business

- One Purpose

- One Body

- Don't Ever, Ever, Ever Give Up

RETREAT SESSION 2

Sessions 3–4

𝔸 = Ask & Listen // ℕ = Never Compromise

Teaching Outline:
Scriptures: Luke 11:1-13; Psalm 119:89; Matthew 5:18; Hebrews 4:12;
2 Timothy 4:1-5

I. God gives us permission to be persistent in prayer (Luke 11:5-8).

    A. We are encouraged to "keep asking," "keep searching," and "keep knocking" (Luke 11:9).

    B. The heart of God is faithful and generous to those who ask (Luke 11:10-13).

II. God's Word keeps us true to Him and to ourselves. It is true and eternal (Psalm 119:89; Matthew 5:18).

    A. God's Word helps us discern the kind of people we need to be in life (Hebrews 4:12).

    B. God's Word helps us decide the path we need to take in life (2 Timothy 4:1-5).

Video Introduction:
For retreat session 2, you will view videos for sessions 3 and 4 on the DVD-ROM.

- Play Video 3 — A = Ask & Listen (11:14)
- Play Video 4 — N = Never Compromise (13:21)

Parents Activity:
I shared in the video that early on at the ranch I would call everyone together to pray when times were tough. I never shared anything that was inappropriate for my family or employees to hear. But I did want them to know, in general terms, when there were some pressing financial needs to be met. We needed to come together as a family and trust God for these things.

Work together with other parents in your group to develop a plan to model and implement this kind of asking and listening in your home, in your specific family situation. As you work on your plan, consider how the following two sharing activities might play out in your home. Can you see your family doing these things together? What parts do you think would work? What are you more hesitant to try? What might work better in your situation? What benefits could come to your family from these kinds of conversations? Share your thoughts and be prepared to give and receive input from other parents in the group.

- Call an official family forum. Make sure you have an item of concern ready to share before you pull everyone together. It may be a financial need for your family or someone else's family. It may be a relational issue that needs to be addressed—maybe forgiveness and restoration need to be attained. Regardless of the need, keep it age appropriate for your children. Nothing too heavy. The point of sharing is not to scare, frighten, or stress your children to the point of worry or anxiety. They need to be protected from that kind of stress. Find a way to share the need in an age-appropriate way. Once you have shared, pray to God and ask Him for help.

- After you have asked God to listen to you, turn to your son and ask him if there is something he needs help with. Don't try to force anything out of him. This is just an opportunity you are giving him to share. You are letting him know that you are listening. If he doesn't share anything, that's OK. More times and opportunities will come later. But if he does share a need, take time to listen. Don't try to fix it. And then spend a few minutes in prayer together for that need.

RETREAT SESSION 3

Sessions 5–6

⌗ = Handle Your Business // ◎ = One Purpose

Teaching Outline:
Scriptures: Leviticus 10:1-11; Psalm 84:10; Ephesians 2:10; Psalm 139:14; Philippians 3:7-11

I. We need to handle our business down to the detail (Leviticus 10:1-11).

A. Be aware of the details because they always matter (Leviticus 10:1-2).

B. God wants our attention and affection on Him (Leviticus 10:3).

C. We don't prepare the way for our sons. We prepare our sons for the way (Leviticus 10:8-11).

II. Spending time with God is the best way to find our purpose (Psalm 84:10).

A. God created and understands each one of us personally (Psalm 139:14).

B. The good things we do for God are all a part of His plan from the beginning (Ephesians 2:10).

C. Knowing Jesus puts the "good" and the "bad" in perspective (Philippians 3:7-11).

Video Introduction:

For retreat session 3, you will view videos for sessions 5 and 6 on the DVD-ROM.

- Play Video 5 — H = Handle Your Business (13:20)
- Play Video 6 — O = One Purpose (13:40)

Parents Activity:

Take the rest of your time to partner with a couple of other parents for this exercise. Answer the following questions about your son. Let the other parents contribute to how you can speak purpose and life into your son. It will help you gain ideas on how to verbally encourage your son, and it will also help other parents get to know him.

(1) What activities does your son lose track of time pursuing? How can you speak life and purpose into your son to direct (or redirect) him through that activity?

(2) How does your son contribute to the lives of others, or make his world a better place in some way? How do you encourage him in this endeavor?

(3) In what ways does your son bring laughter to others? How have you seen him bring the good out in others? How can you nurture this in him?

(4) What things does your son talk about wanting to accomplish? In what ways can you speak life into his dream, passion, or goal?

(5) What natural abilities, qualities, or skills does your son possess? What makes him unique? Do you see patterns emerging? How can you verbally support your son and encourage him to use his natural abilities to find his purpose?

RETREAT SESSION 4

Sessions 7–8

Ⓞ = One Body // Ⓓ = Don't Ever, Ever, Ever Give Up

Teaching Outline:
Scriptures: 1 Corinthians 6:19-20; Deuteronomy 6:4-9

I. We are called to honor God with our bodies (1 Corinthians 6:19-20).

    A. We pursue stewardship over ownership of our bodies—they are a gift to us, but they do not belong to us (1 Corinthians 6:19).

    B. The price God paid for us was high (1 Corinthians 6:20).

II. God refuses to give up on His children (Deuteronomy 6:4-9).

    A. God has promised Himself to us, and we should pledge ourselves to Him (Deuteronomy 6:4-6).

    B. Parents who pursue their children for God also pave the way for their sons to pursue Him for themselves (Deuteronomy 6:7-9).

Video Introduction:
For retreat session 4, you will view videos for sessions 7 and 8 on the DVD-ROM.

- Play Video 7 — O = One Body (10:31)
- Play Video 8 — D = Don't Ever, Ever, Ever Give Up (13:49)

Parents Activity:

Find a couple of other parents to huddle up with and brainstorm ideas together for age-appropriate activities that you can partner with your son to complete. Once you get home, do the same thing with your son—brainstorm together and agree on an activity. Some examples include:

- Plant a small garden (or potted garden plants) and grow some vegetables. Be sure to involve your son in the maintenance.

- Start collecting a series of coins, baseball cards, model cars, etc. that can be given to another person for birthday or Christmas.

- Design the ideal tree house, and then build a miniature version of it with wooden tongue depressors.

- Partner with your son in prayer about a long-term concern that he will understand—maybe the annual standardized testing at school for him and/or a project at work or home for you. Every week or so, talk about the challenges that you are currently facing, then make the determination to stick with it, do your best, and not give up.

The point is to bring into focus the idea that some things take a long time to accomplish. This project needs to be long enough to communicate this idea to your son without exhausting you both in the process. Throughout the progress of this activity and even at the conclusion of it, talk about how it felt to want to quit or give up. Then talk about how God never has given up on us.

LEADER GUIDE

We're glad you have chosen to take your small group through *The Two-Minute Drill to Parenting*. As this study guides your group members through a game plan to help ensure their sons are ready for authentic manhood, it is our prayer that they will not only feel empowered to become a more godly influence but they will also experience a closer relationship with their sons as they share this journey together. Before you get started, here is some helpful information about the different elements you'll encounter within the study.

Week Introduction

Each session begins with an overview of the week's topic. This material is designed to help you introduce the topic of study for the week. You will want to read this before your group meets so that you'll better understand the context for your time together. For weeks 2-8, suggest that group members read this introduction before you meet.

Huddle Up: Review

This time is designed to provide group members with an opportunity to talk about what God has been revealing to them or what insights have resulted from their personal time during the week.

Huddle Up: Preview

Your actual group time will most likely begin here with an icebreaker that is designed to help you ease into the study and get everyone talking. These questions are intended to be nonthreatening to group members so that a pattern of participation can be established early on.

Video Discussion

This section provides an overview of what your group will experience through the video message as well as discussion questions related to its content. This is an opportunity for your group to discuss specific aspects of the message, what they heard, and how they were affected.

Small-Group Discussion

This portion of your weekly group meeting will not only reinforce the video content but also take your group deeper into the truth of the Scriptures. This segment of the study also gives group members an opportunity to integrate these truths into their own parenting.

NOTE: The Small-Group Discussion portion of your meeting each week is built around four types of questions. You may find it helpful to familiarize yourself with these:

Observation—What is this passage telling us?

Observation questions help group members identify what the biblical text is saying. Asking this type of question usually causes members to look back at the passage in order to discover the answer.

Interpretation—What does the passage mean?

The purpose of an interpretation question is to discover what the text means. While each passage has many applications, it only has one interpretation. These questions cause the group to wrestle with the meaning of a verse or passage.

Application—Now that I know what I know, what will I do to integrate this truth into my life?

Application questions help group members see how they can act on the principle they discovered in the passage. Good application questions will help people to think, *What should I do about this?* We are bringing the truth back into our culture/context and applying it here and now.

Self-Revelation—How am I doing in light of the truth unveiled?

Self-revelation questions require the reader to assess personal progress in applying the truth. This is the most intimately revealing question to ask. We are identifying to what degree we are living the truth.

Highlights

This section serves as a conclusion to the group time and summarizes key points from your small-group meeting each week.

Execute the Play

At the end of each session you will find a suggested activity for group members to complete during the week. This activity is an opportunity for them to take what they've learned during your small-group meeting and apply it. They may be asked to involve their son or to complete an activity in preparation for a future conversation with him. During the next group meeting they will have time to share some of what they've learned with your group during the Review time.

SESSION 1: THE GAME PLAN

Week Introduction

Welcome group members to the study and make sure everyone has a member book. You may want to have a marker and name tags on hand (just for the first week), especially if it's a group that's new to each other. Consider jumping to the Huddle Up: Preview section first this week and then introducing the topic for Session 1.

Huddle Up: Review

In weeks 2-8 this time will be used to talk about what God has been revealing to them or what insights have resulted from their personal time during the week. But for the first session, take a few moments for the group to share any personal goals they have for this study. Be ready to share your own goals to get the conversation going.

Huddle Up: Preview

Give everyone an opportunity to answer the question that introduces this week's topic—fashioning a game plan for their sons. The icebreaker will get the group thinking about the topic in general terms. Encourage all group members to share during this time. Some members will be more comfortable speaking aloud than others. Just remember that the objective is to give everyone the opportunity to get involved.

Video Discussion

Play the video for Session 1 (10:53). Encourage group members to listen closely as John, his wife Tee, and others talk about parenting, discipline, and what it looks like to create an effective game plan for raising their sons. Encourage them to take additional notes when they hear something that resonates with them. After the video concludes, take time to answer the questions provided on these pages. If you have a larger group, break them into smaller groups for the first question or two. Then bring everyone back together for the final question in this section of the study. This time will give your group members an opportunity to discuss specific aspects of the message, what they heard, and how they were affected.

Small-Group Discussion

After the group has completed the video discussion, you will lead them right into the small-group discussion time. Before your meeting, check the Leader Helps on the DVD-ROM in your leader kit for additional group discussion guidance. We have taken each question and provided an explanation for why it is included as well as examples of possible responses when appropriate.

In this session you will examine ways the culture of the "real world" affects your sons and what you can do to combat that influence as well as how sharing you life lessons can help move your sons toward manhood.

Highlights

If time allows, spend a few minutes summarizing the group session by using the bullet points provided in this section. Conclude your group time in prayer. For the first week, you should be the one to pray aloud. In the coming weeks, when your group gets more comfortable, consider asking volunteers to pray.

Execute the Play

Encourage group members to complete the activity in this section before your next group meeting. Remind them that they will have a chance to talk about what God has shown them through this experience.

Finally, share that next week you will be looking at the foundational step that will lead their sons toward manhood—choosing the right kind of Master for their lives.

SESSION 2: M=MASTER

Week Introduction

Welcome group members back. Use the narrative overview to help you introduce the topic of study for Session 2. Make sure you read this before your group meets so you'll better understand the topic and context for your time together.

Huddle Up: Review

Before you move forward, take a moment to review last week. Talk about ideas they came up with for a transition trip. If someone is stuck, allow other group members an opportunity to share ideas.

Huddle Up: Preview

Give everyone an opportunity to answer the questions. Continue to encourage all group members to share during this time.

Video Discussion

Play the video for Session 2 (11:09). Encourage group members to listen closely for helpful information about the choices their sons make, obedience to Christ, and modeling Christ in front of their kids. After the video concludes, take time to answer the questions provided on these pages. If you have a larger group, break them into smaller groups for the first question or two. Then bring everyone back together for the final question in this section of the study. This time will give your group members an opportunity to discuss specific aspects of the message, what they heard, and how they were affected.

Small-Group Discussion

After the group has completed the video discussion, you will lead them right into the small-group discussion time. Before your meeting, check the Leader Helps on the DVD-ROM in your leader kit for additional group discussion guidance.

In this session you will talk about the first step in developing manhood—choosing the right Master.

Highlights

If time allows, spend a few minutes summarizing the group session by using the bullet points provided in this section. Conclude your group time in prayer. This week you may consider asking a volunteer to lead the prayer. If you lead the prayer, ask God to give group members the strength they need to help their sons choose the right Master to be in charge of their lives.

Execute the Play

Encourage group members to complete the activity in this section before your next group meeting. Remind them that they will have a chance to talk about what God has shown them through this experience.

Share that next week you will be talking about what it looks like for a real man to ask and listen to God.

SESSION 3: 𝔸 = ASK & LISTEN

Week Introduction

Welcome group members back. Use the narrative overview to help you introduce the topic of study for Session 3. As always, make sure you read this before your group meets so that you'll better understand the topic and context for your time together.

Huddle Up: Review

Start your small-group session by looking back at last week. Talk about what they discovered about themselves as they examined how the things they say they value really line up with how they spend their time, resources, and energy. Encourage group members to speak up about how God has inspired or challenged them this week.

Huddle Up: Preview

Give everyone an opportunity to answer the questions. Continue to encourage all group members to share during this time.

Video Discussion

Play the video for Session 3 (11:14). Encourage group members to listen closely for helpful information about asking God for direction and really listening to Him. After the video concludes, answer the questions provided on these pages. If you have a larger group, break into smaller groups for the first question or two. Then bring everyone back together for the final question. This time will give group members an opportunity to discuss specific aspects of the message, what they heard, and how they were affected.

Small-Group Discussion

After the group has completed the video discussion, you will lead them right into the small-group discussion time. Before your meeting, check the Leader Helps on the DVD-ROM in your leader kit for additional group discussion guidance.

In this session you will talk about how to ask and listen to God as well as how important it is for your sons to see you, as the parent, ask God for help.

Highlights

If time allows, spend a few minutes summarizing the group session by using the bullet points provided in this section. Conclude your group time in prayer, asking God to help you as you model the lessons from this session for your sons.

Execute the Play

Encourage group members to complete the activity in this section before your next group meeting. Remind them that they will have a chance to talk about what God has shown them through this experience.

Share that next week you will be talking about the importance of being consistent and following through with what God has asked you to do.

SESSION 4: Ｎ = NEVER COMPROMISE

Week Introduction

Welcome group members back. Use the narrative overview to help you introduce the topic of study for Session 4. Make sure you read this before your group meets so that you'll better understand the topic and context for your time together.

Huddle Up: Review

Start your small-group session by looking back at last week. Talk about what they learned from their "Ask & Listen" Family Forum time. Encourage group members to speak up about how God has inspired or challenged them this week.

Huddle Up: Preview

Give everyone an opportunity to answer the questions. Continue to encourage all group members to share during this time.

Video Discussion

Play the video for Session 4 (13:21). Encourage group members to listen closely for helpful information about how easy it is for compromise to settle into our lives unnoticed. After the video concludes, answer the questions provided on these pages. If you have a larger group, break into smaller groups for the first question or two. Then bring everyone back together for the final question. This time will give group members an opportunity to discuss specific aspects of the message, what they heard, and how they were affected.

Small-Group Discussion

After the group has completed the video discussion, you will lead them right into the small-group discussion time. Before your meeting, check the Leader Helps on the DVD-ROM in your leader kit for additional group discussion guidance.

In this session you will look more closely at the only real, true remedy for compromise and inconsistent actions—to go to God's Word and let it examine us.

Highlights

If time allows, spend a few minutes summarizing the group session by using the bullet points provided in this section. Conclude your group time in prayer. Ask for a volunteer to start the prayer. As the leader, close the prayer time by asking God to help you all live lives of consistency, refusing to compromise.

Execute the Play

Encourage group members to complete the activity in this section before your next group meeting. Remind them that they will have a chance to talk about what God has shown them through this experience.

Share that next week you will be talking about the importance of teaching your sons to be responsible and handle their own business.

SESSION 5: 𝕳 = HANDLE YOUR BUSINESS

Week Introduction

Welcome group members back. Use the narrative overview to help you introduce the topic of study for Session 5. Make sure you read this before your group meets so that you'll better understand the topic and context for your time together.

Huddle Up: Review

Before you move forward, take a moment to review last week. Give group members an opportunity to talk about a time when they met a problem head on or a time when they failed to do so. Encourage them to give each other feedback on how they can use their stories to teach their sons about never compromising.

Huddle Up: Preview

Give everyone an opportunity to answer the questions. This activity will give group members a chance to identify how they first learned about responsibility themselves. Encourage all group members to share.

Video Discussion

Play the video for Session 5 (13:20). Encourage group members to listen closely for the five things John considers non-negotiable when it comes to handling our business. After the video concludes, take time to answer the questions provided on these pages. If you have a larger group, break into smaller groups for the first question or two. Then bring everyone back together for the final question. This time will give group members an opportunity to discuss specific aspects of the message, what they heard, and how they were affected.

Small-Group Discussion

After the group has completed the video discussion, lead them right into the small-group discussion time. Before your meeting, check the Leader Helps on the DVD-ROM in your leader kit for additional group discussion guidance.

In this session you will talk about the importance of preparing your sons for the way instead of preparing the way for your sons.

Highlights

If time allows, spend a few minutes summarizing the group session by using the bullet points provided in this section. Conclude your group time in prayer. Ask for a volunteer to open your prayer time and open the floor for anyone to pray who would like to. Close the prayer time, asking God to help you be good examples for your sons in your work ethic and the way you manage time and finances.

Execute the Play

Encourage group members to complete the activity in this section before your next group meeting. Remind them that they will have a chance to talk about what God has shown them through this experience.

Share that next week you will be talking about the importance of teaching your sons to pursue God and *His* purpose for their lives.

SESSION 6: ⓪ = ONE PURPOSE

Week Introduction

Welcome group members back. Use the narrative overview to help you introduce the topic of study for Session 6. Make sure you read this before your group meets so that you'll better understand the topic and context for your time together.

Huddle Up: Review

Before you move forward, take a moment to review last week. Give group members an opportunity to talk about helping their sons budget for a goal. Ask them about any impact they observed as their sons realized that through hard work and discipline their goals were attainable.

Huddle Up: Preview

Give everyone an opportunity to answer the questions. Continue to encourage all group members to share during this time.

Video Discussion

Play the video for Session 6 (13:40). Encourage group members to listen closely for helpful information about finding their purpose in God and what that looks like. After the video concludes, take time to answer the questions provided on these pages. If you have a larger group, break into smaller groups for the first question or two. Then bring everyone back together for the final question. This time will give group members an opportunity to discuss specific aspects of the message, what they heard, and how they were affected.

Small-Group Discussion

After the group has completed the video discussion, lead them right into the small-group discussion time. Before your meeting, check the Leader Helps on the DVD-ROM in your leader kit for additional group discussion guidance.

In this session you will talk about helping shape who your sons are going to be, not who you want them to be as well as modeling obedience to God for your sons.

Highlights

If time allows, spend a few minutes summarizing the group session by using the bullet points provided in this section. Conclude your group time in prayer. Give group members an opportunity to pray and thank God for the opportunity they have to introduce their sons to Christ.

Execute the Play

Encourage group members to complete the activity in this section before your next group meeting. Remind them that they will have a chance to talk about what God has shown them through this experience.

Share that next week you will be talking about how to help your sons develop a healthy, well-rounded, biblical view of their bodies.

SESSION 7: Ⓞ = ONE BODY

Week Introduction

Welcome group members back. Use the narrative overview to help you introduce the topic of study for Session 7. Make sure you read this before your group meets so that you'll better understand the topic and context for your time together.

Huddle Up: Review

Before you move forward, take a moment to review last week. Give group members an opportunity to discuss how much they think their sons understand about what it takes to really *know* someone. Talk also about what next steps they plan for helping their sons *know* Jesus Christ on a personal level.

Huddle Up: Preview

Take turns answering the questions. This activity turns the discussion toward how our culture promotes a body-conscious mindset. Encourage all group members to share.

Video Discussion

Play the video for Session 7 (10:31). Encourage group members to listen closely for helpful information about what it means to take care of our bodies, as well as how to teach our sons to show proper respect for girls and their bodies. After the video concludes, take time to answer the questions provided on these pages. If you have a larger group, break into smaller groups for the first question or two. Then bring everyone back together for the final question. This time will give group members an opportunity to discuss specific aspects of the message, what they heard, and how they were affected.

Small-Group Discussion

After the group has completed the video discussion, lead them right into the small-group discussion time. Before your meeting, check the Leader Helps on the DVD-ROM in your leader kit for additional group discussion guidance.

In this session you will discuss the difference between ownership and stewardship of our bodies as well as the specific purpose of our bodies—to be used for God and His purposes.

Highlights

If time allows, spend a few minutes summarizing the group session by using the bullet points provided in this section. Have someone close the group in prayer or conclude yourself. If you lead the prayer, ask God to guide each of you in teaching your sons how to treat their bodies with respect.

Execute the Play

Encourage group members to complete the activity in this section before your next group meeting. Remind them that they will have a chance to talk about what God has shown them through this experience.

Share that next week you will be talking about the influence you have on your sons when it comes to how they respond to adversity in life. You'll also talk about what is next for your group when you complete your study of *The Two-Minute Drill to Parenting*, so encourage group members to think about what they would like to see happen.

SESSION 8: D = DON'T EVER, EVER, EVER GIVE UP

Week Introduction

Welcome group members back for your last session. Use the narrative overview to help you introduce the topic of study for Session 8. Make sure you read this before your group meets so that you'll better understand the topic and context for your time together.

Huddle Up: Review

Before you move forward, take a moment to review the previous week. Let group members use this time to talk about the ways their sons have made them more active. Also encourage those who have older sons to share about their "king and queen" conversations.

Huddle Up: Preview

Give everyone an opportunity to answer the questions. The first question will provide an opportunity for the movie buffs in the group to have some fun while the second question will give everyone a chance to think about what most motivates them to persevere.

Video Discussion

Play the video for Session 8 (13:49). Encourage group members to listen closely to what John has to say about what it takes to be the kind of parent—regardless of the circumstances—who refuses to quit. After the video concludes, take time to answer the questions provided on these pages. If you have a larger group, break into smaller groups for the first question or two. Then bring everyone back together for the final question. This time will give group members an opportunity to discuss specific aspects of the message, what they heard, and how they were affected.

Small-Group Discussion

After the group has completed the video discussion, lead them right into the small-group discussion time. Before your meeting, check the Leader Helps on the DVD-ROM in your leader kit for additional group discussion guidance.

In this session you will talk about teaching your sons that commitment is a choice, and so is giving up. You will also look at how choosing to never give up on your son is modeling who God is to him as well.

Highlights

If time allows, spend a few minutes summarizing the group session by using the bullet points provided in this section. Conclude your group time in prayer. Thank God for this eight-week journey you have just completed together. When all have prayed who wish to, close the prayer by asking God to help you put into practice all you have learned. Pray that group members will walk away from this study not only feeling empowered to become more godly influences but that they will also experience a closer relationship with their sons as they move forward.

Execute the Play

Encourage group members to complete the activity in this section even though you won't come together again as a group to discuss it. Suggest that they take some extra time to reflect on what they have learned through this study of *The Two-Minute Drill to Parenting*.

Before everyone gets away, talk about what's next for your group. If you want to stay together and do another study, check out lifeway.com/smallgroups for options. You might also consider splitting into two groups to make room for new members.

GROUP DIRECTORY

Name: _____
Home Phone: _____
Mobile Phone: _____
E-mail: _____
Social Networks(s): _____
_____

Name: _____
Home Phone: _____
Mobile Phone: _____
E-mail: _____
Social Networks(s): _____
_____

Name: _____
Home Phone: _____
Mobile Phone: _____
E-mail: _____
Social Networks(s): _____
_____

Name: _____
Home Phone: _____
Mobile Phone: _____
E-mail: _____
Social Networks(s): _____
_____

Name: _____
Home Phone: _____
Mobile Phone: _____
E-mail: _____
Social Networks(s): _____
_____

Name: _____
Home Phone: _____
Mobile Phone: _____
E-mail: _____
Social Networks(s): _____
_____

Name: _____
Home Phone: _____
Mobile Phone: _____
E-mail: _____
Social Networks(s): _____
_____

Name: _____
Home Phone: _____
Mobile Phone: _____
E-mail: _____
Social Networks(s): _____
_____

Name: _____
Home Phone: _____
Mobile Phone: _____
E-mail: _____
Social Networks(s): _____
_____

Name: _____
Home Phone: _____
Mobile Phone: _____
E-mail: _____
Social Networks(s): _____
_____

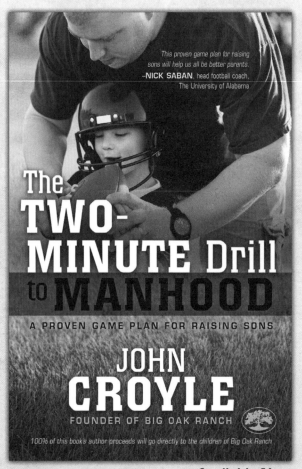

JOHN CROYLE

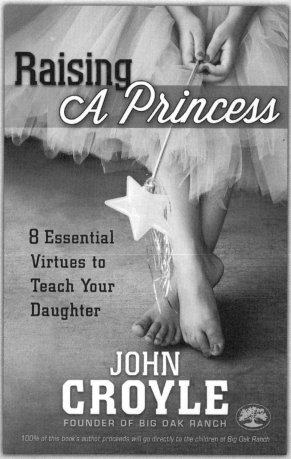

Coming May 2014

Raising A Princess begins with the end in mind. The end is the Proverbs 31 woman; Croyle keeps her squarely in view as he looks at what parenting techniques help the reader to raise a princess who will someday be a queen.

Every WORD matters
BHPublishingGroup.com